Cultural Arts in Columbus Book Series Vol 1

Walk in Short North Columbus Ohio
Short North Art District
Shoichiro Nakamura

Printed by CreateSpace, Available at Amazon.com
Published in 2017
ISBN-13: 978-1546766957

About Short North

Short North is a district along High Street in the city of Columbus, which stretches from near north of downtown to the south of the Ohio State University campus. Approximately half of Short North near down town is named Short North Art District, which is flourishing with a large number of art galleries, fashionable stores, restaurants, and night clubs. The other half near the OSU campus, named Gate Way, is now the most vibrant construction area with construction of new stores and apartments.

However, Short North was once a distressed area in suburbanization period of 1960-1970 when affluent people moved to suburbs. In this period, indeed, old building in the area were inhabited by poor people or abandoned with windows boarded. In the same period, downtown was too in similar conditions except the small business area in the center of downtown.

The city government of Columbus worked hard to revitalize the down town and the Short North area. Some notable effort included the construction of a three story shopping mall named City Center on the south side of Ohio Theater, which once attracted many shoppers, but later popularity quickly declined, and demolished unfortunately. Another effort was to move COSI to the west side of Scioto river called Franklinton area, which was successful.

Revitalization of Short North near downtown started in the beginning of 1980's, when a number of art galleries opened in the area. The tax credits by the city assisted attracting business and gallery owners. The Short North Business Association founded soon sought funding from the City of Columbus and transform the area into a thriving community. In 1999, the Short North Special Improvement District (SID) was established to improve the safety, cleanliness, and beauty of the District.

Gallery Hop in Short North sponsored by ALIVE, CD102.5, and the Greater Columbus Arts Council opens every Saturday between 4-10pm. Thousands of people gather in Short North to visit new gallery exhibitions, street performances, and special events. Restaurants and bars open until late.

This book is a collection of the photos taken in Short North Art District. The murals and street arts in Short North are covered in the companion book, *Mural and Street Arts in Columbus OH, Part 1 Short North and Downtown*.

North High Street and Ohio Center Way Area

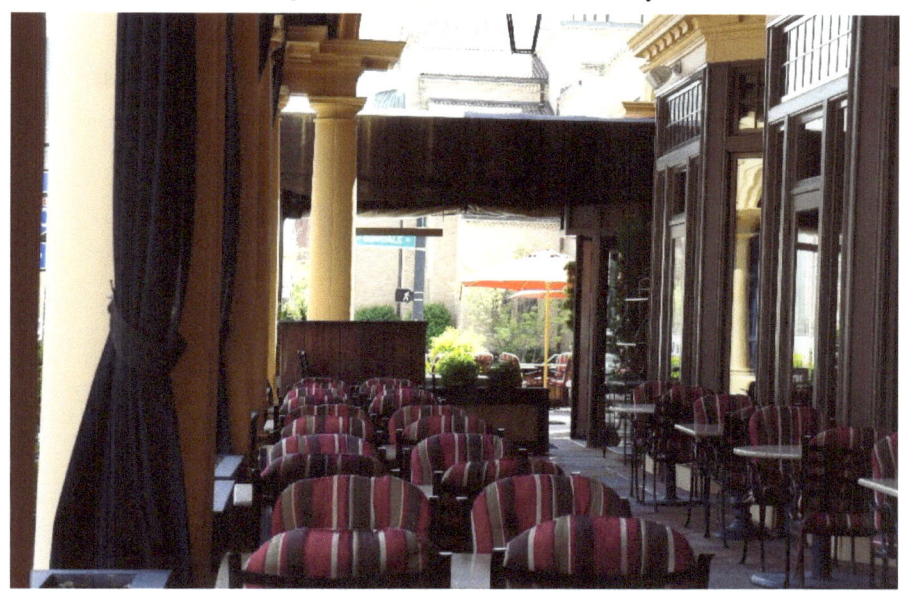

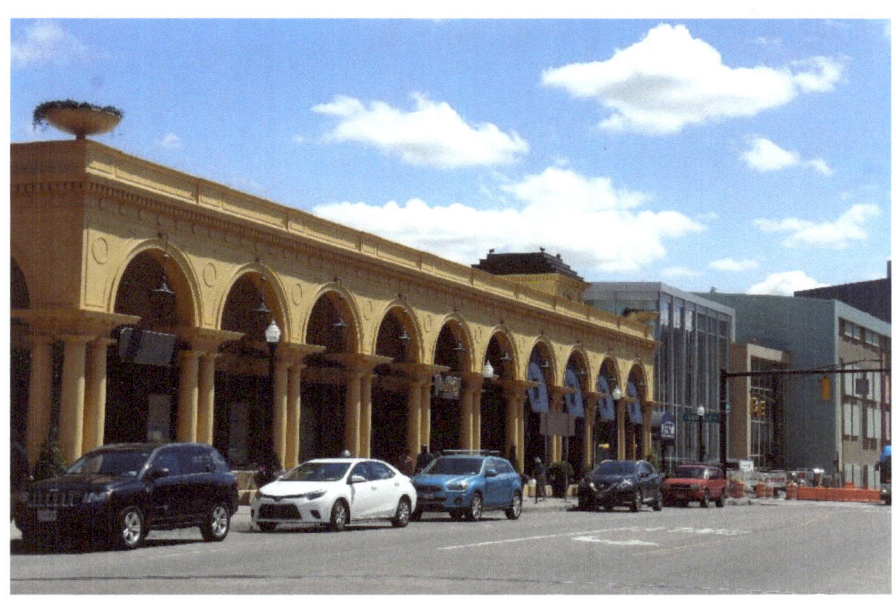

Convention Center

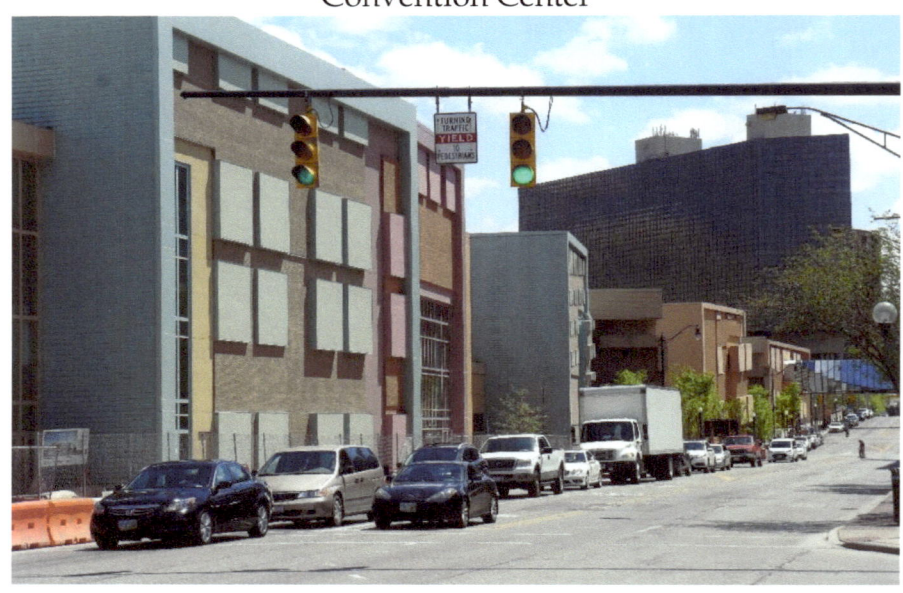

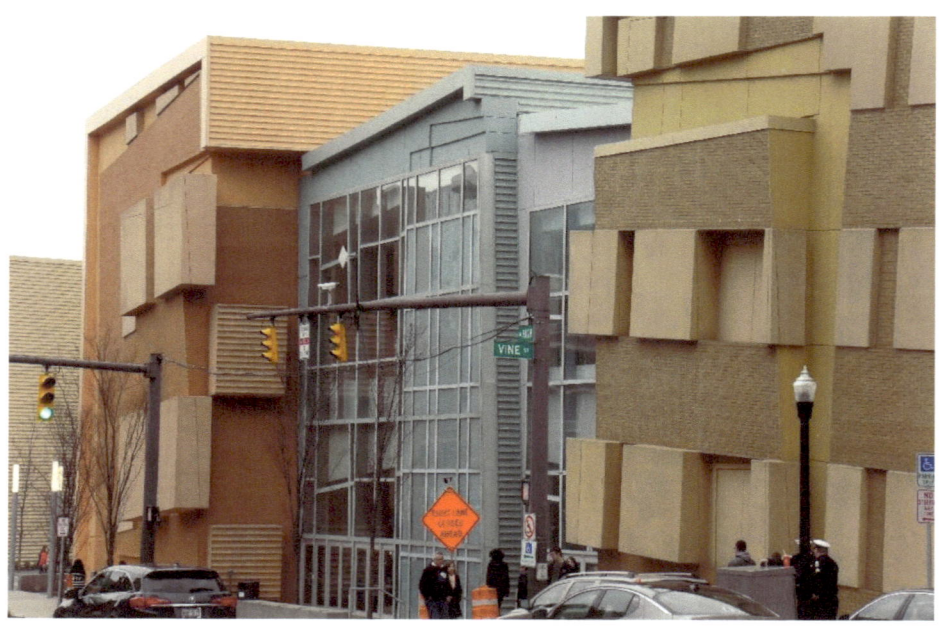

GM Corvair displayed in Convention Center

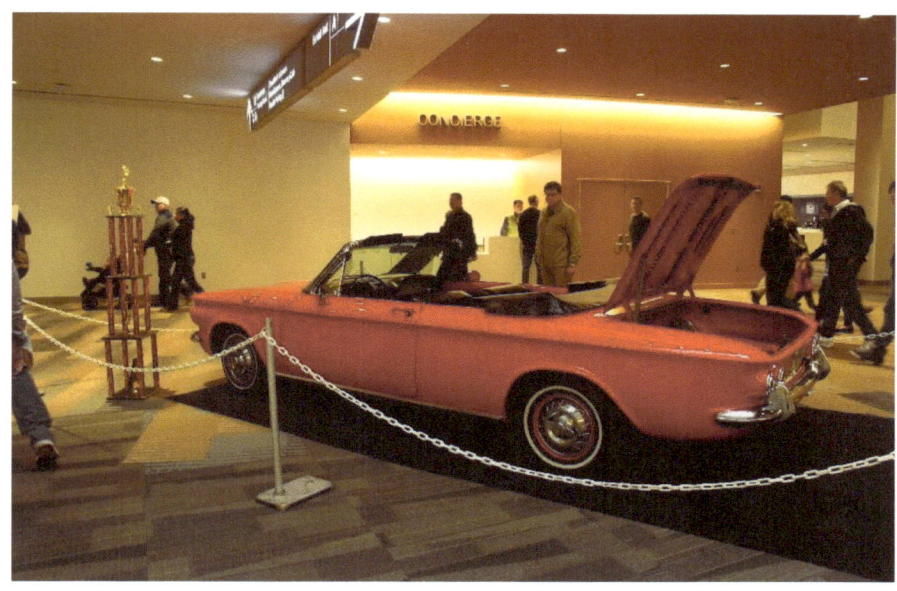

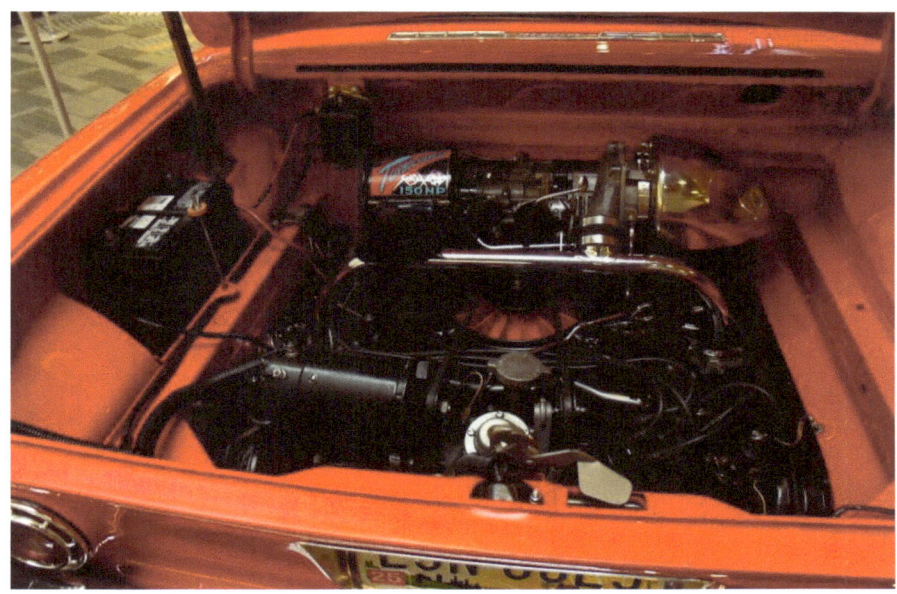

Interior decorations of Convention Center

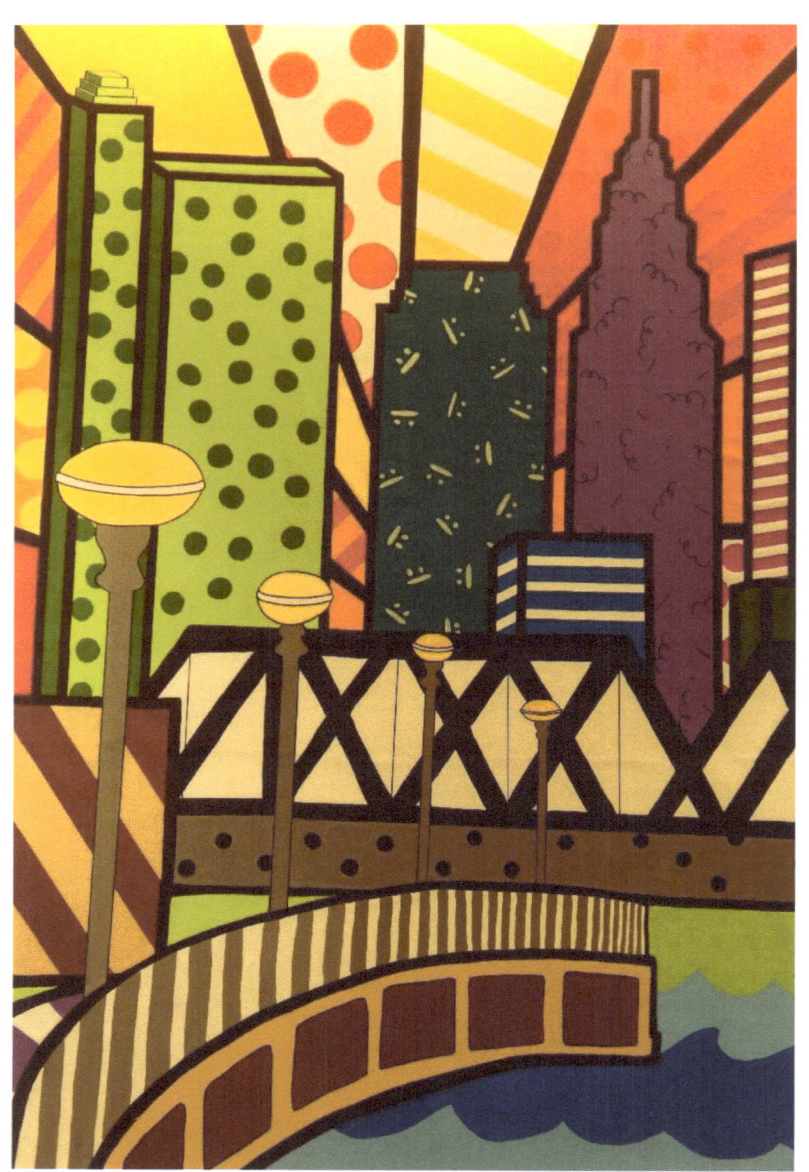

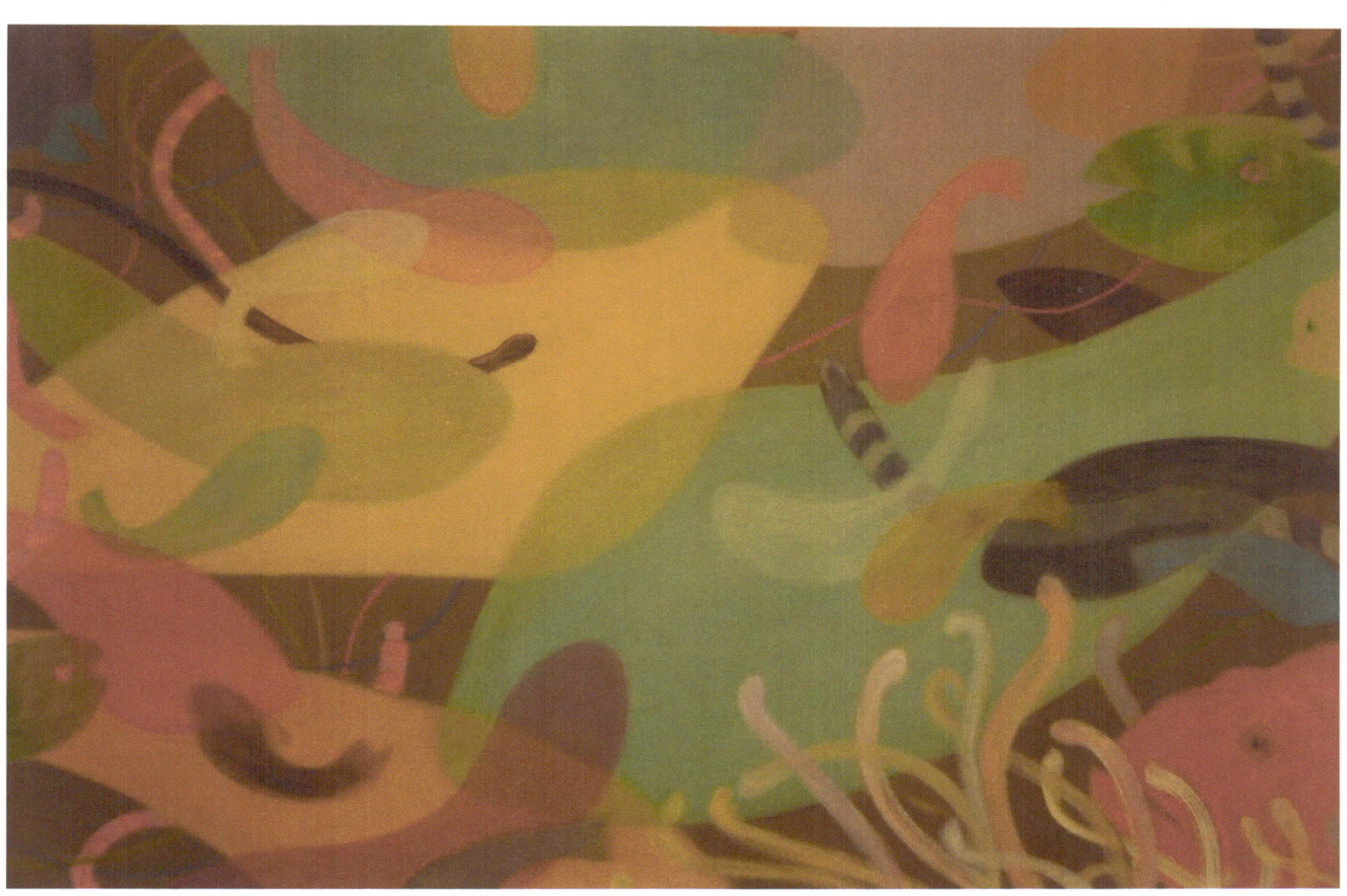

Hilton Columbus Downtown

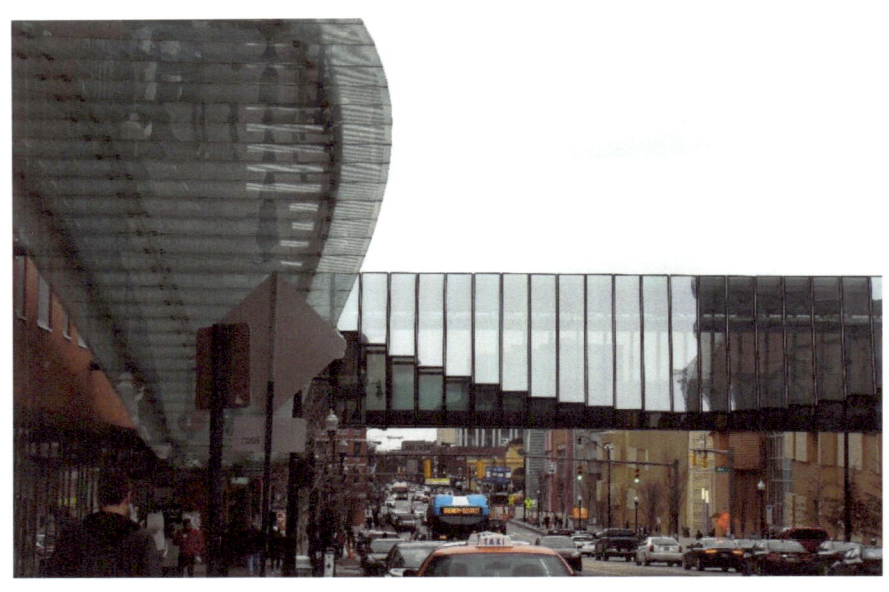

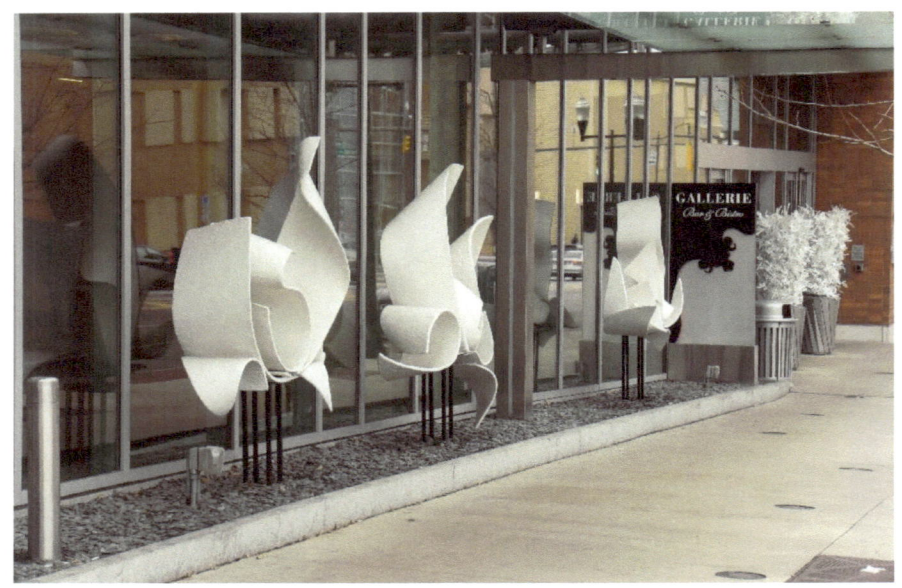

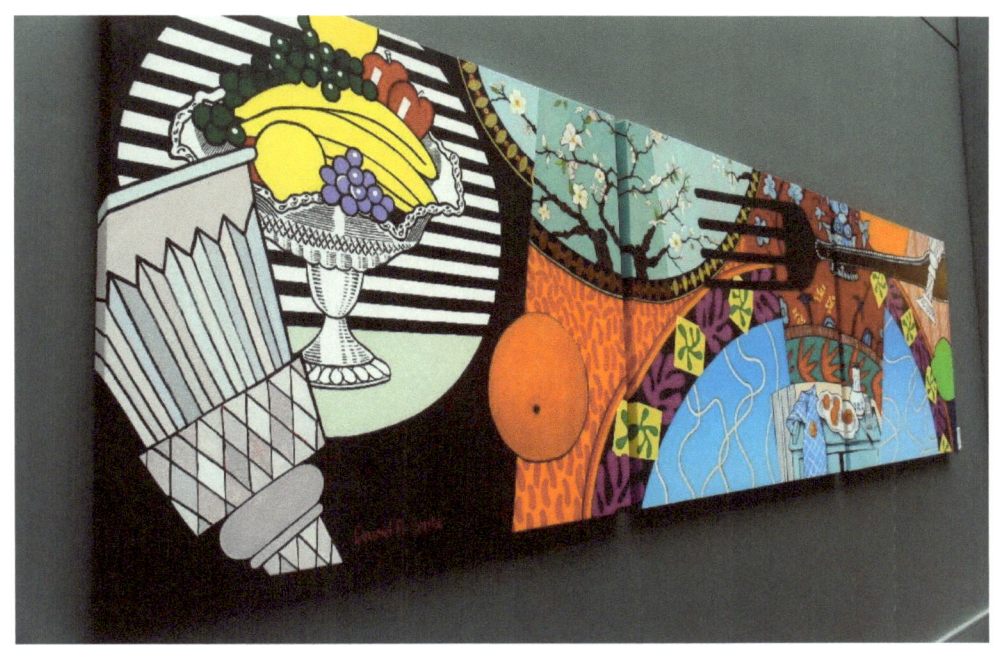

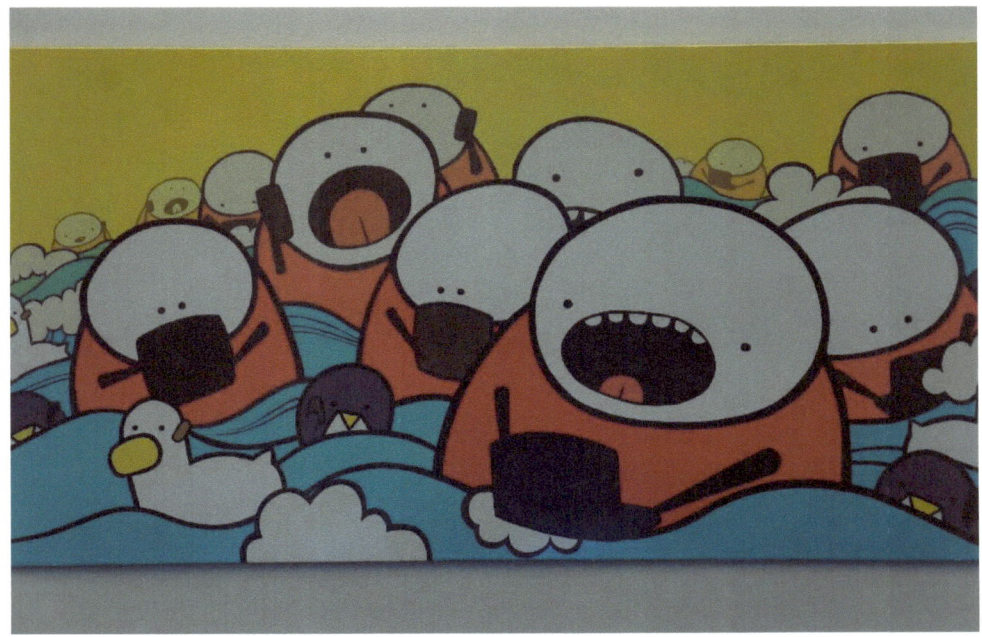

A boutique store

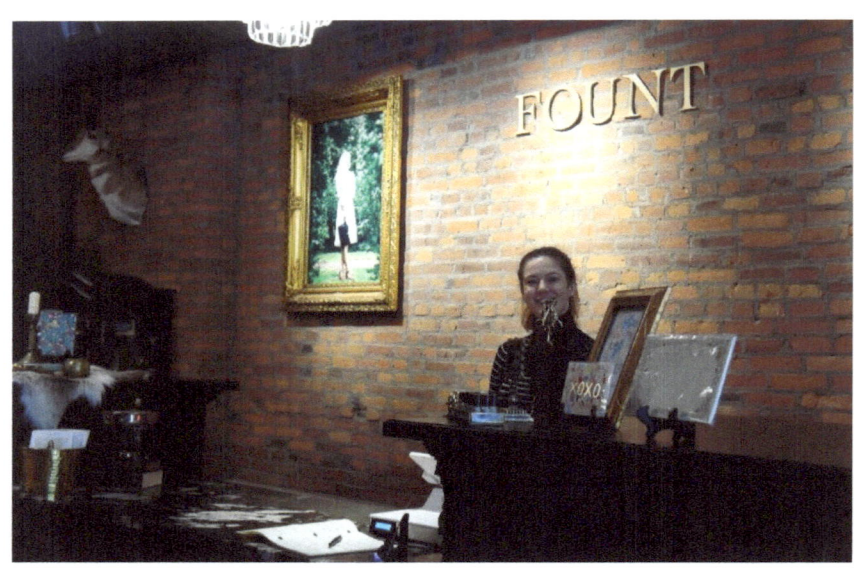

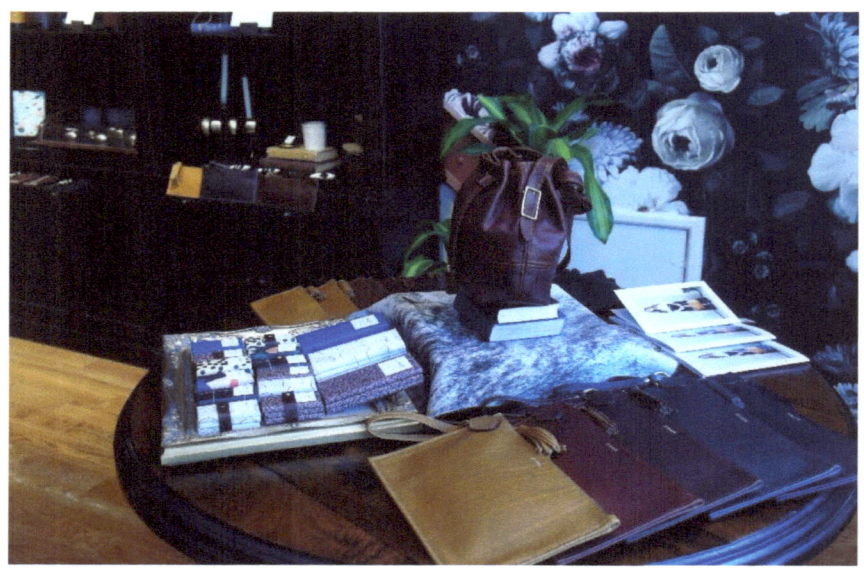

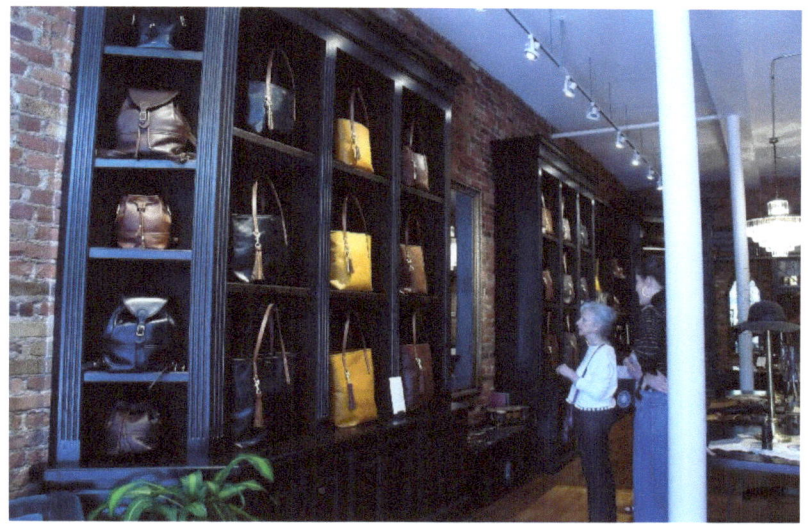

Short North Neighborhood

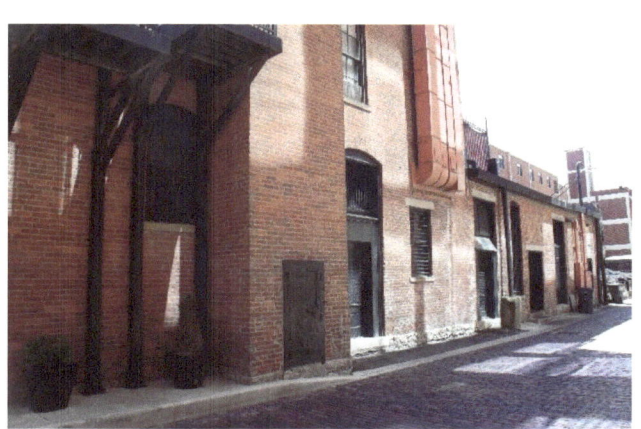

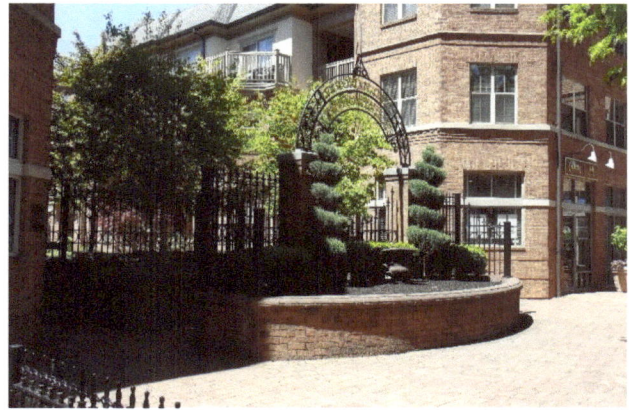

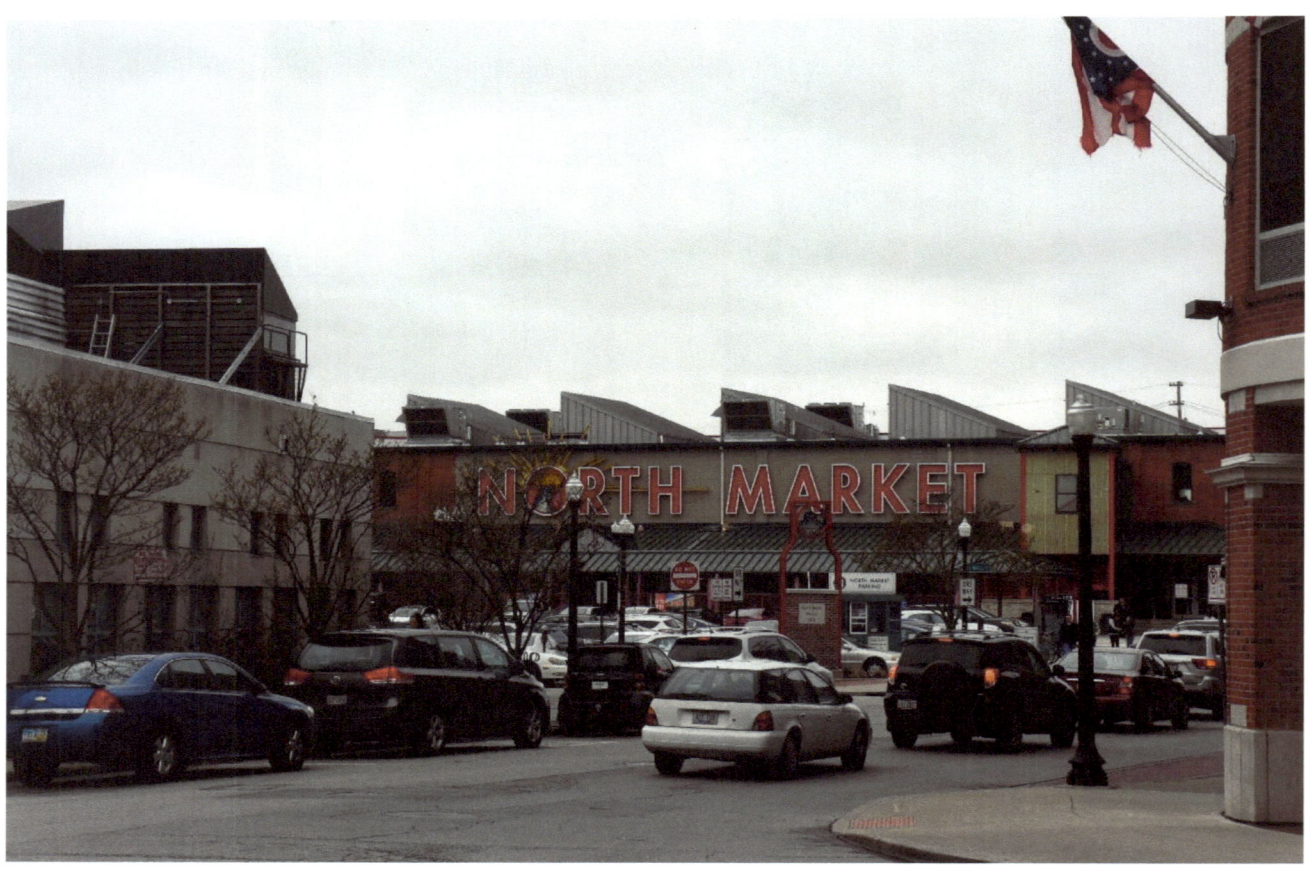

An Apparel Store

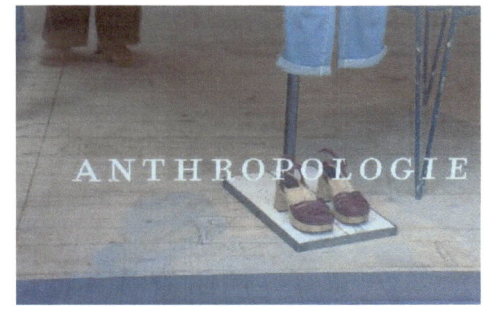

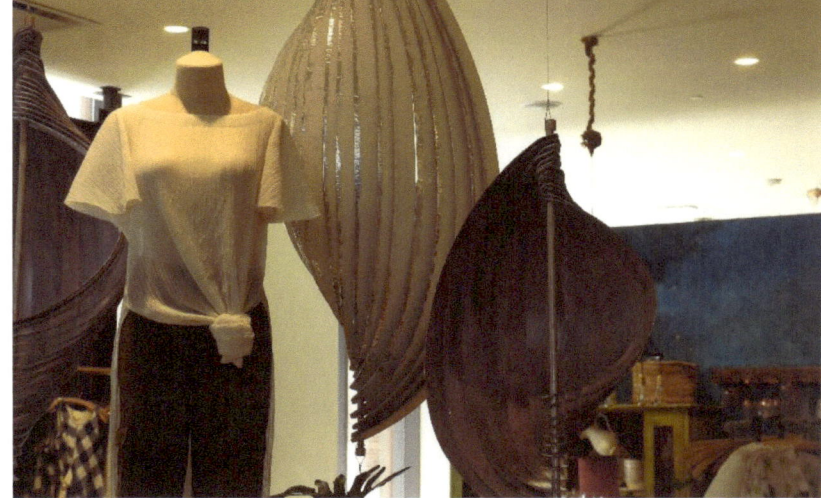

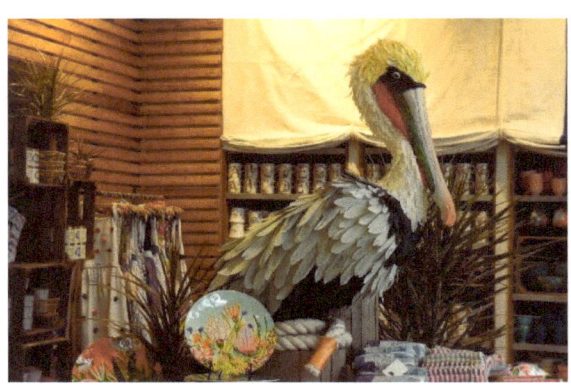

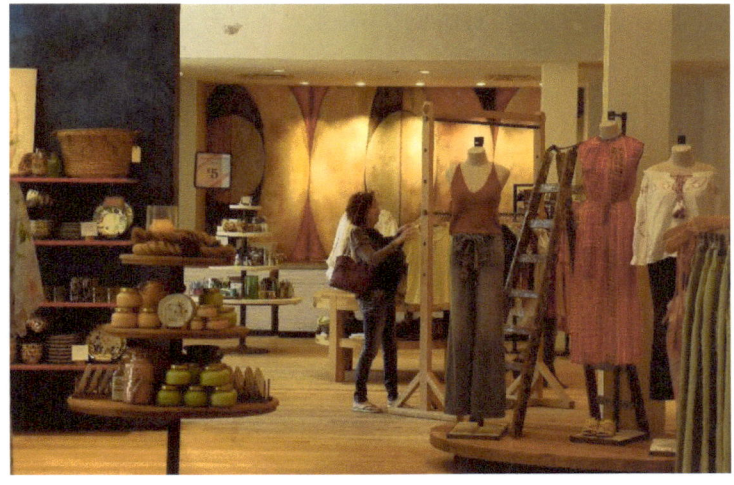

Street Views

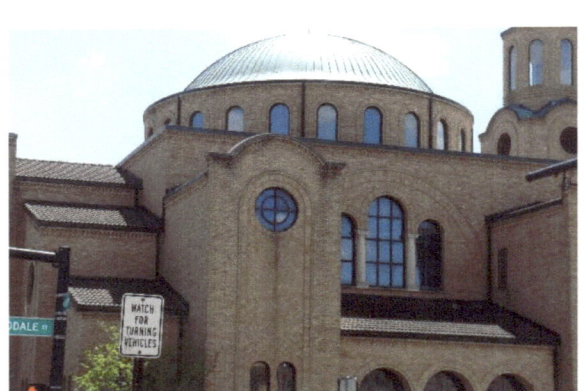

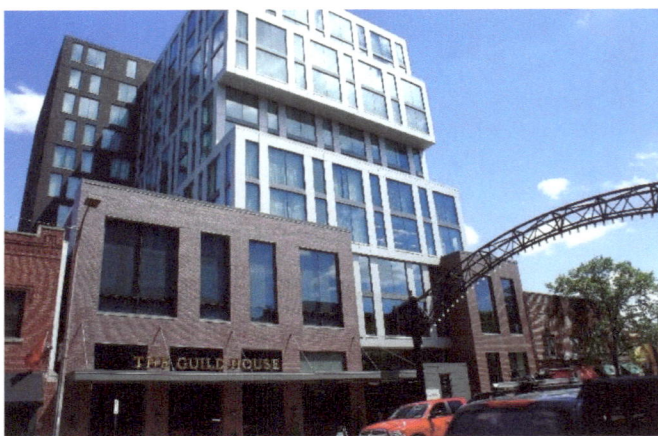

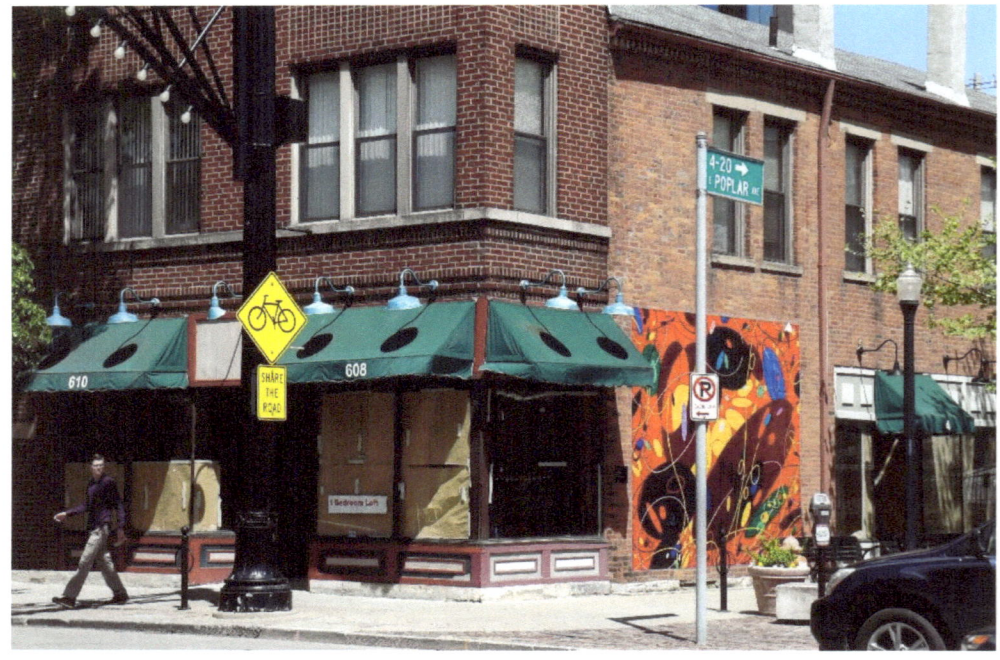

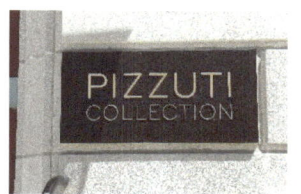

Pizzuti Collection gallery

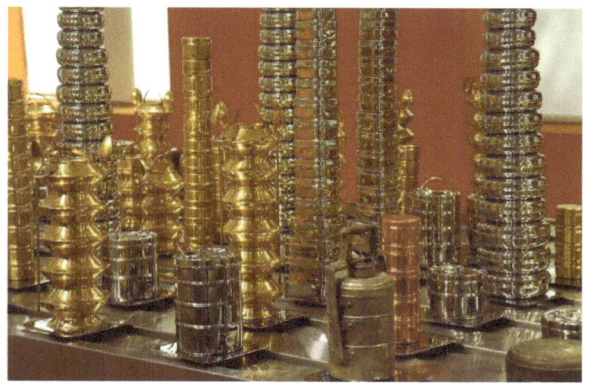

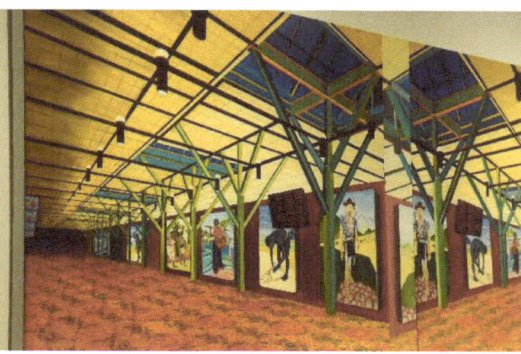

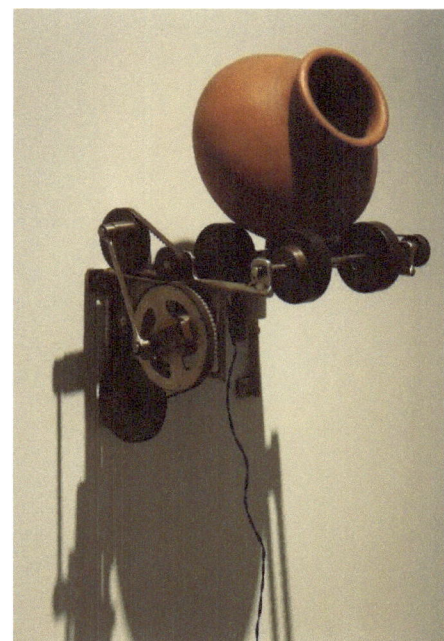

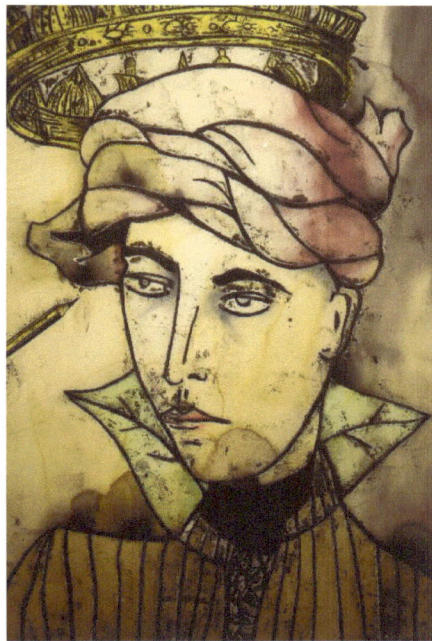

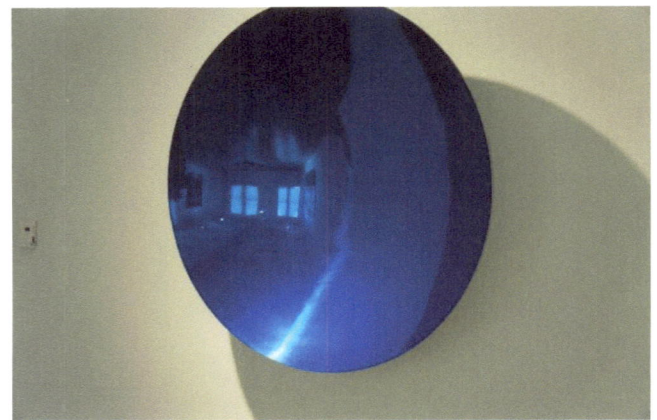

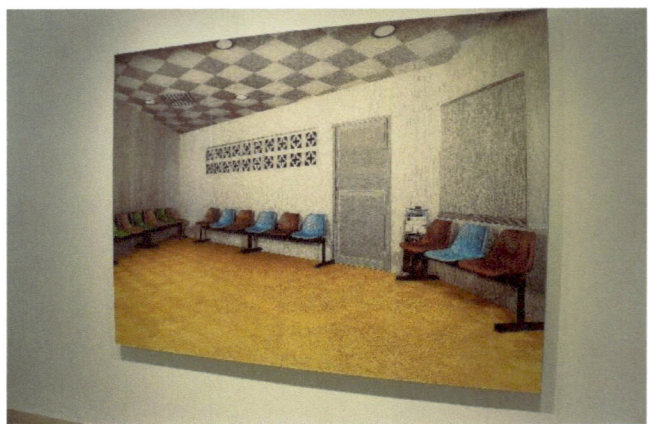

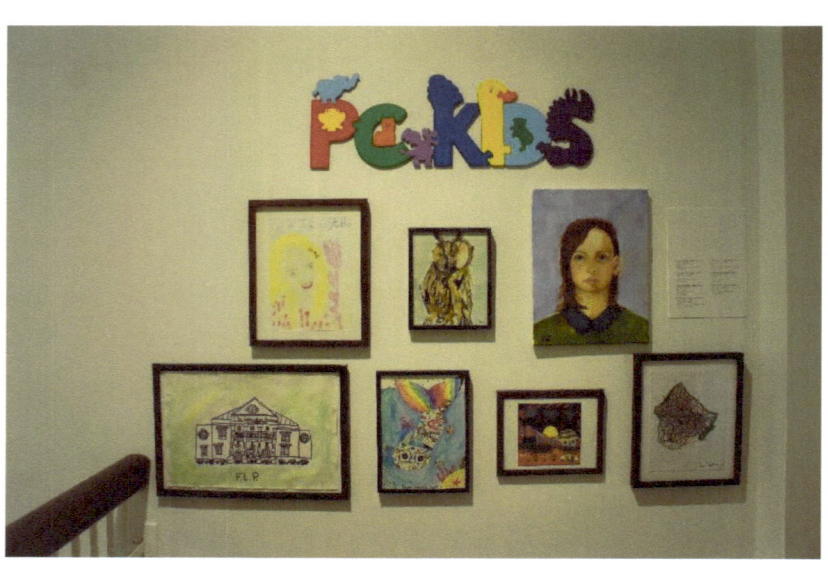

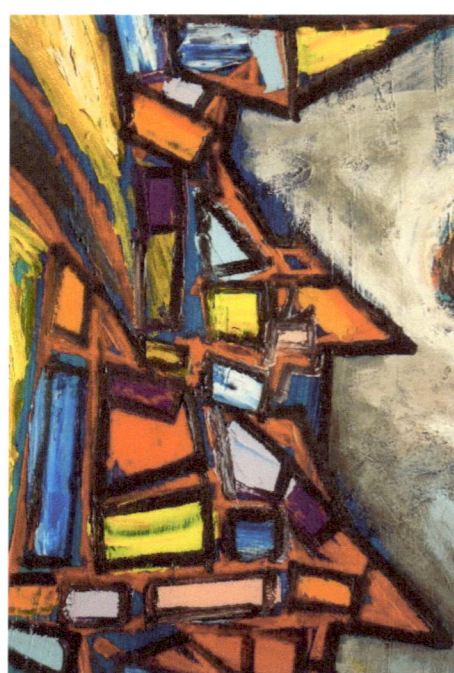

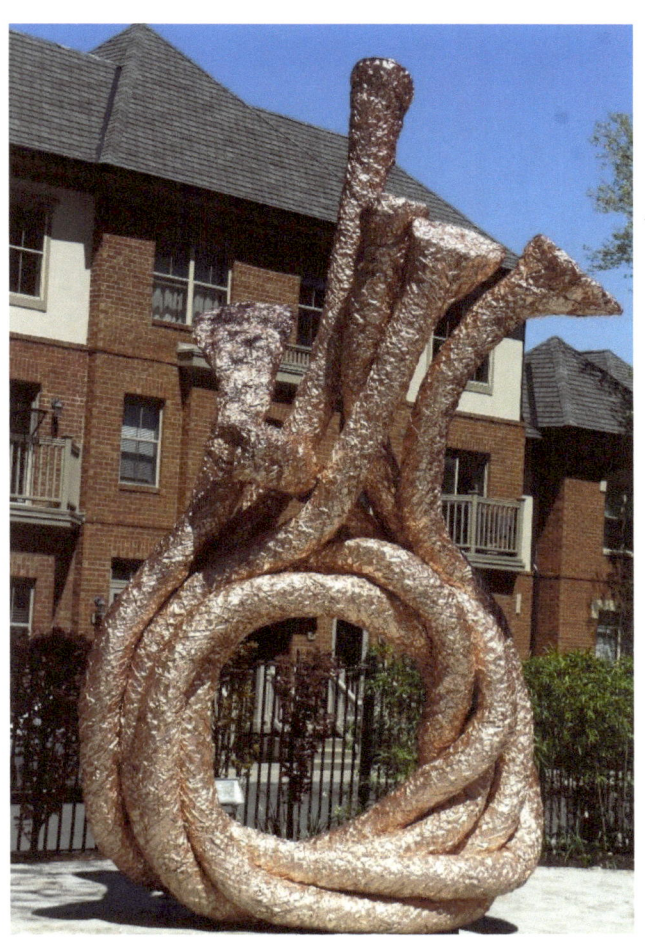

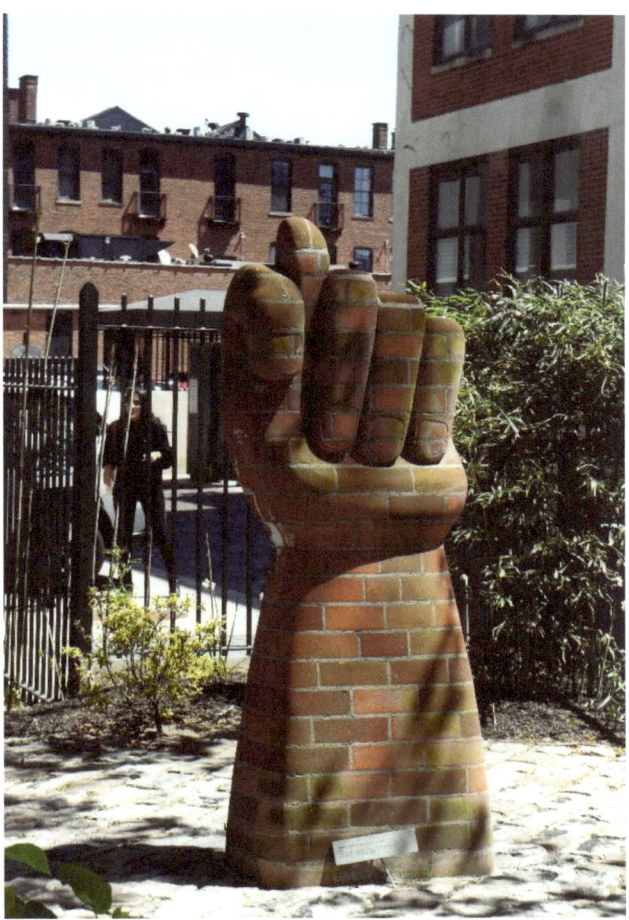

A bank with unusual inside decoration

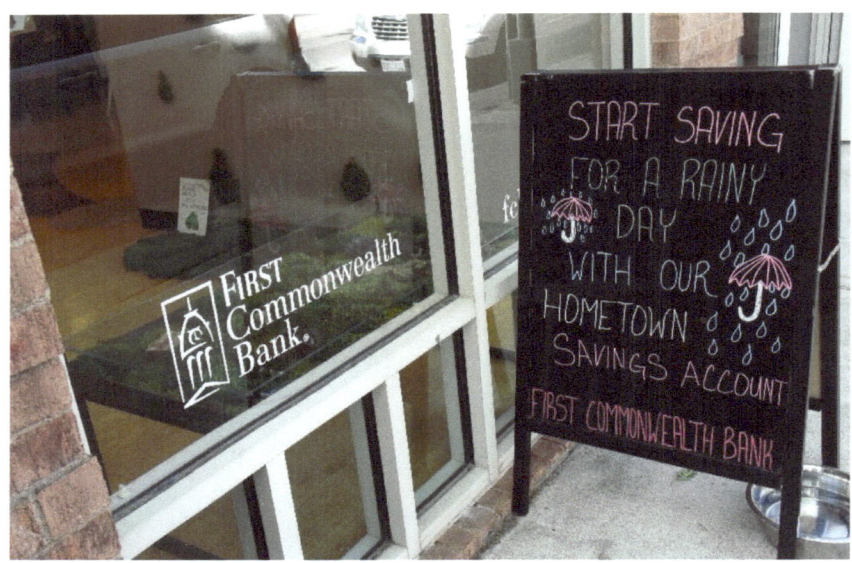

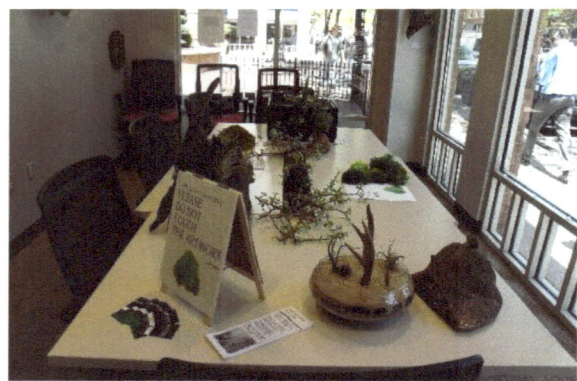
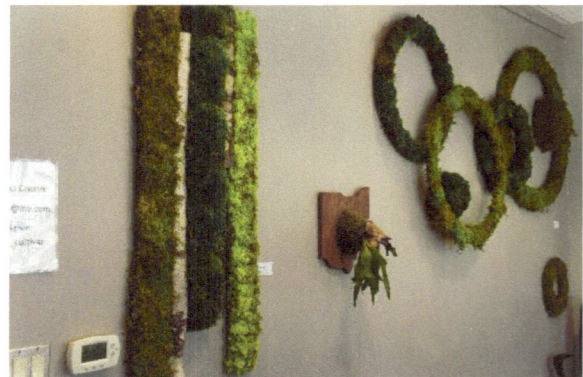

Galleries

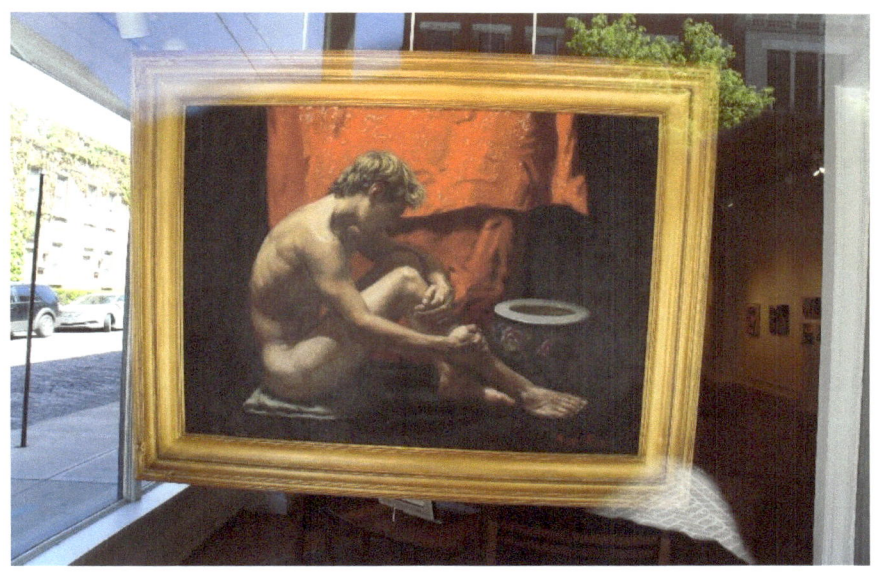

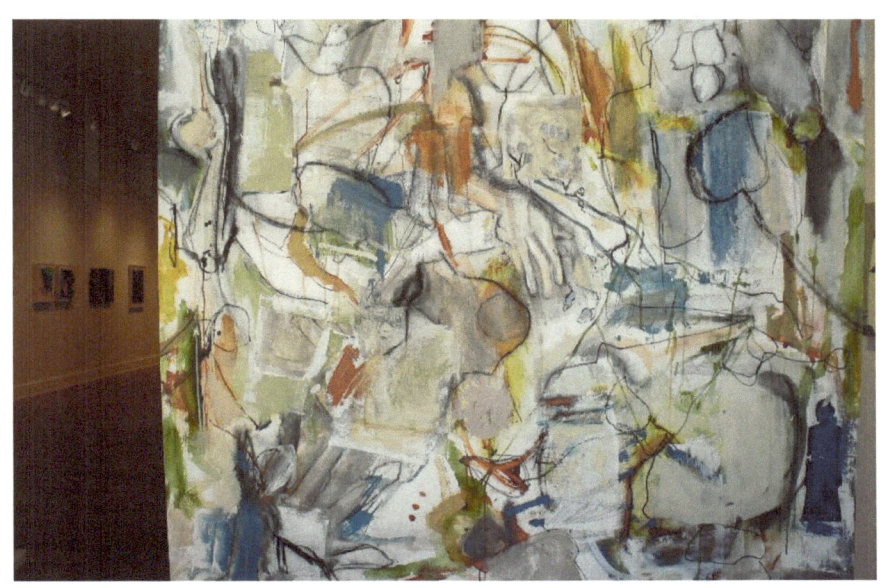

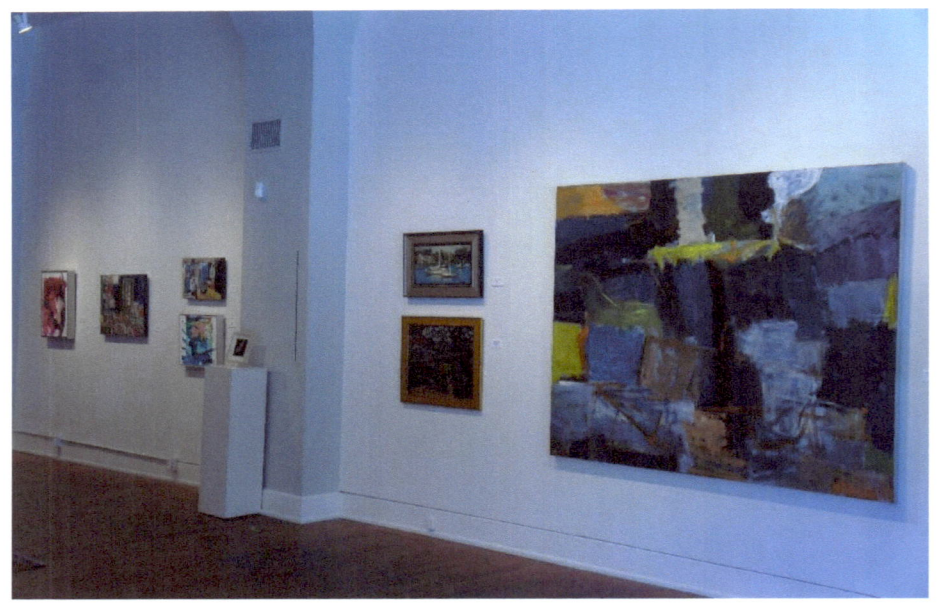

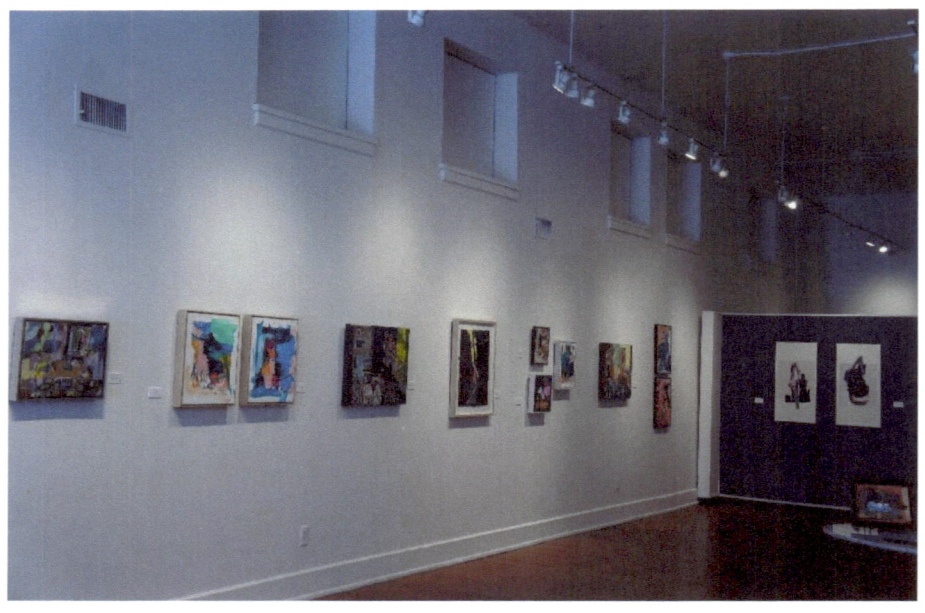

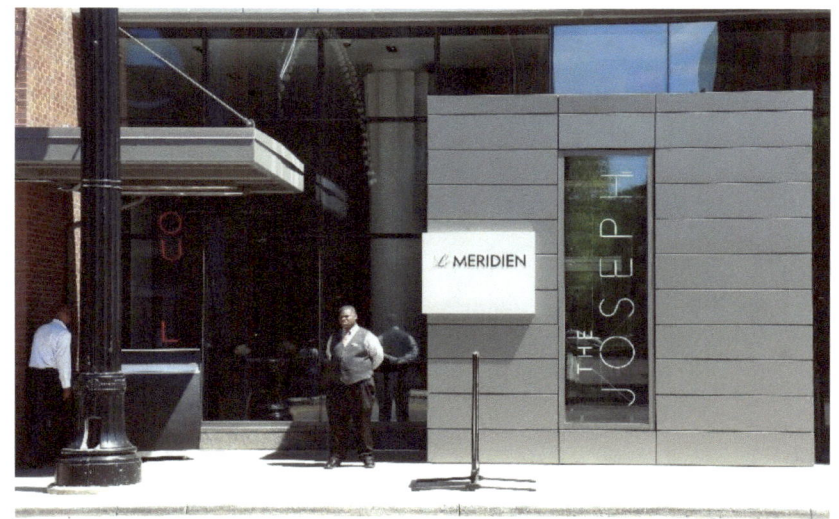

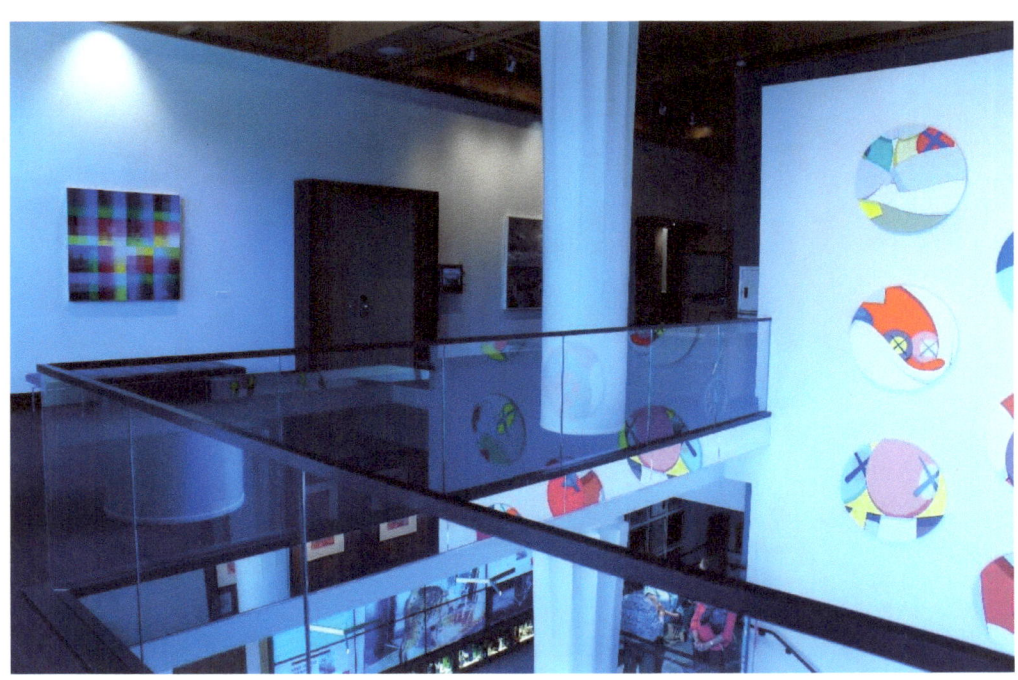

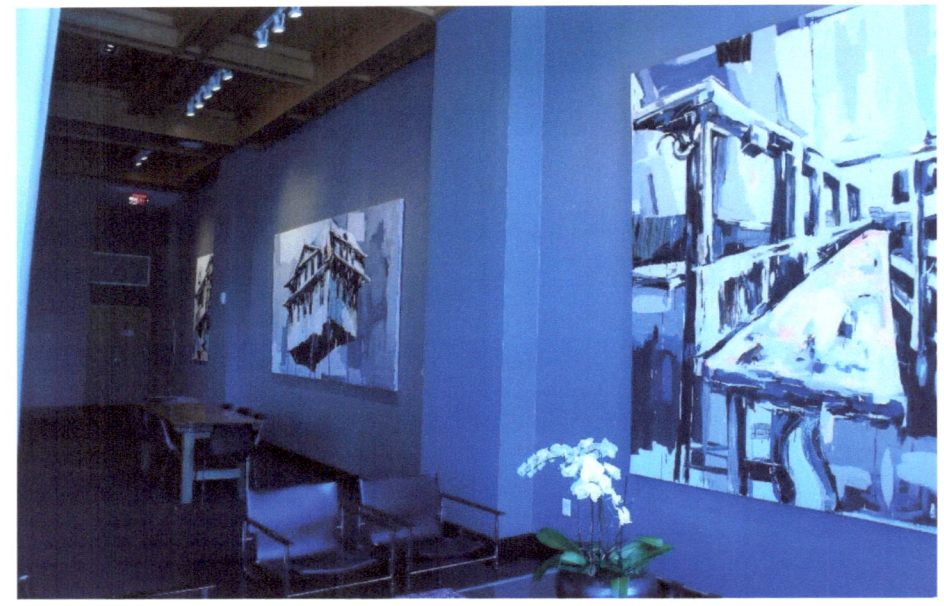

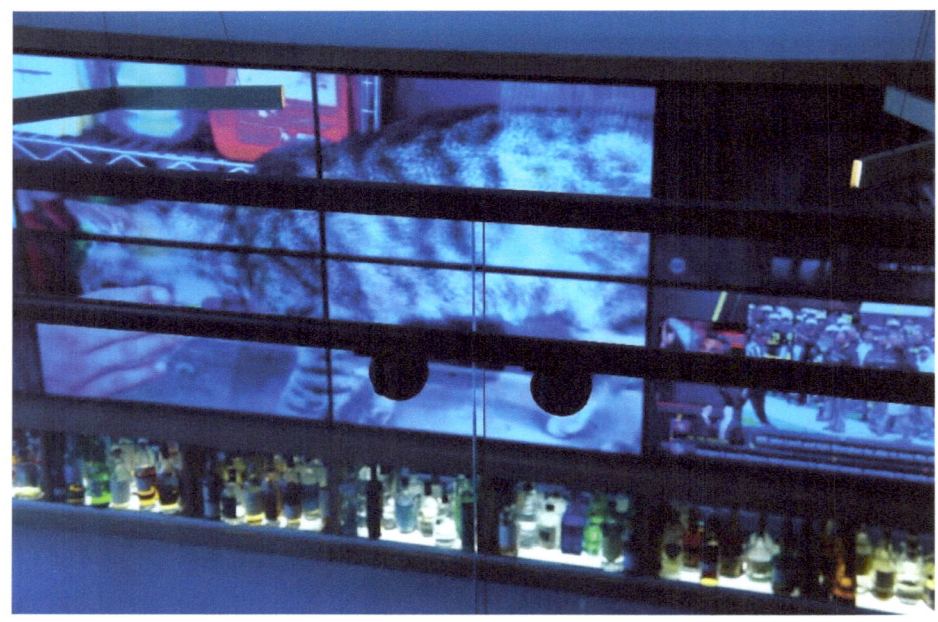

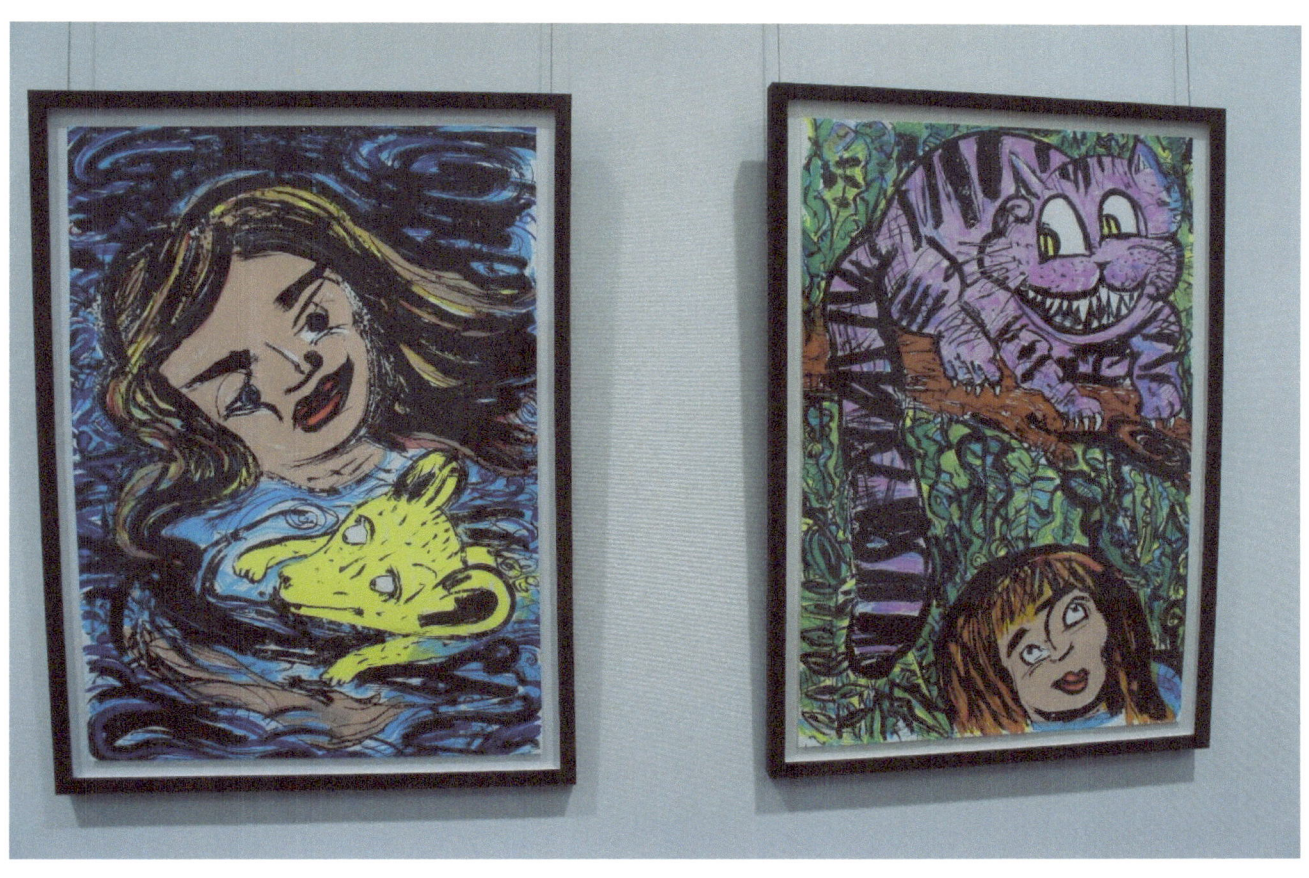

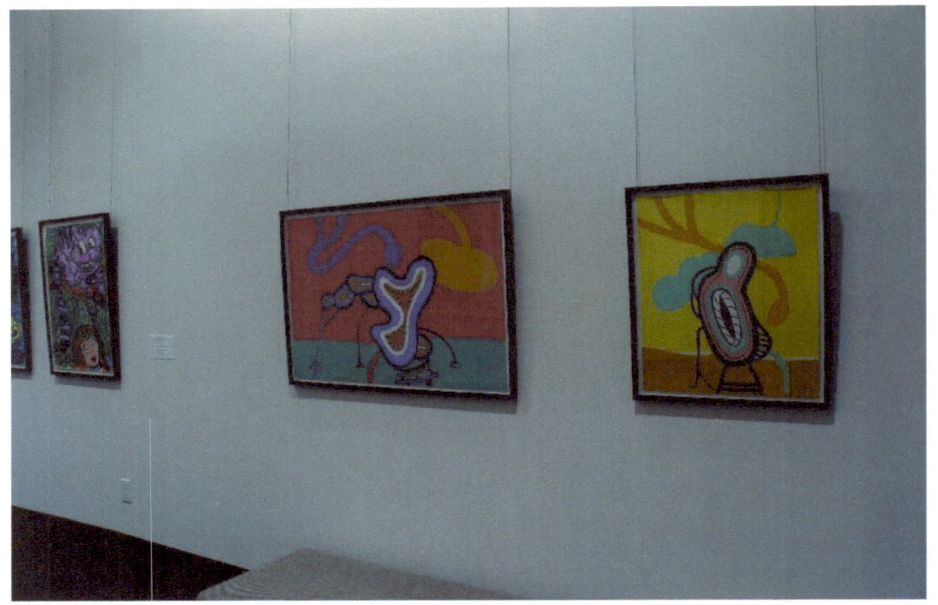

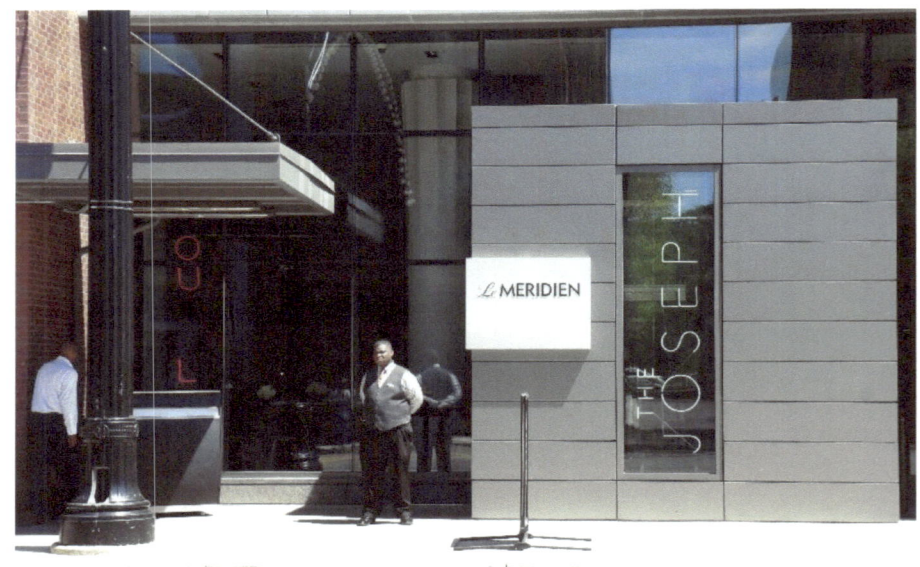

Restaurant Veracino decorated with the ceramic garden

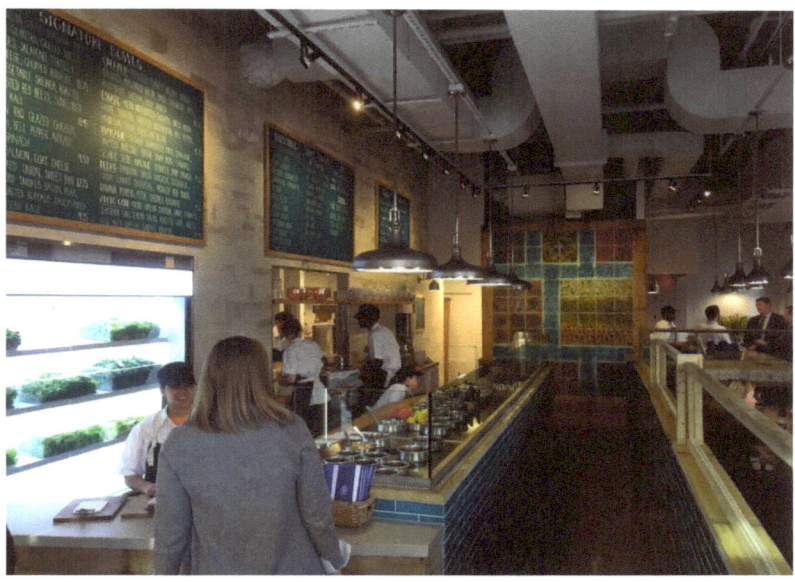

Night view of High Street

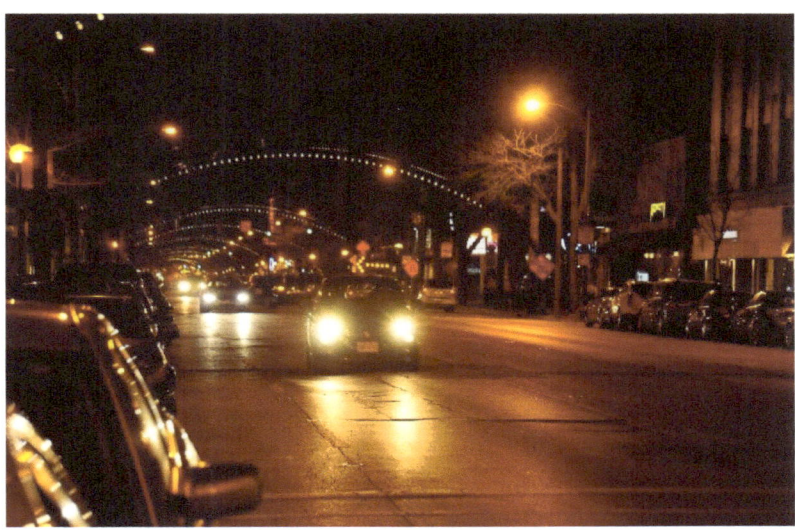

Note Cards and Large Prints

Note card (greeting card) and large print of the photos in this book can be ordered by sending what are to be ordered by email to ismr.us However this service is limited to United State customers only.

The cost of one note card is $6 (shipping free) including envelop enclosed in cellophane bag. To order card(s), write in the email the page number of the photo in this book (and which photo if multiple), and how many cards are desired. Any number of photos or card for each photo can be ordered. An invoice will be returned to which a payment may be done securely by Paypal or credit card. Once the payment is finished it will take about a week until the products are mailed to the customer.

For large print(s) please send to

Cultural Arts in Columbus Book Series

Vol 1   Walk in Short North of Columbus OH
Vol 2   Murals and Street Arts in Columbus OH
            Part 1 Shot North and Downtown
Vol 3   Murals and Street Arts in Columbus OH
            Part 2   Franklinton (Forthcoming)

www.ingramcontent.com/pod-product-compliance
Lightning Source LLC
Chambersburg PA
CBHW041307180526
45172CB00003B/1003